THE SCIENCE OF
ICE HOCKEY

By
Emilie Dufresne

KidHaven PUBLISHING

PLAY
SMART

Published in 2021 by
KidHaven Publishing, an Imprint of Greenhaven Publishing, LLC
353 3rd Avenue
Suite 255
New York, NY 10010

Cataloging-in-Publication Data

Names: Dufresne, Emilie.
Title: The science of ice hockey / Emilie Dufresne.
Description: New York : KidHaven Publishing, 2021. | Series: Play
smart | Includes glossary and index.
Identifiers: ISBN 9781534535688 (pbk.) | ISBN 9781534535701
(library bound) | ISBN 9781534535695 (6 pack) | ISBN
9781534535718 (ebook)
Subjects: LCSH: Hockey--Juvenile literature. | Sports sciences--
Juvenile literature.
Classification: LCC GV847.25 D847 2021 | DDC 796.962--dc23

Printed in the United States of America

CPSIA compliance information: Batch #BS20K: For further information contact
Greenhaven Publishing LLC, New York, New York, at 1-844-317-7404.

Please visit our website, www.greenhavenpublishing.com.
For a free color catalog of all our high-quality books,
call toll free 1-844-317-7404 or fax 1-844-317-7405.

Find us on

Photo credits:

Cover – ChrisVanLennepPhoto, Ronnie Chua, Vereshchagin Dmitry, Longchalerm Rungruang, Grushin. 2 - AlenaLitvin. 4 - Idea
Studio. 5 - Ronnie Chua. 6 - B Calkins. 7 - Pressmaster. 8 - terekhov igor. 9 - GrashAlex. 10 - Iurii Osadchi. 11 - Iurii Osadchi. 12 -
kataonia82.13 - Anton Gvozdikov. 14 - Andrey Yurlov. 15 - mexrix. 16 - DarioZg. 17 - mexrix. 18 - Pukhov K. 19 - Eugene Onischenko.
20 - Lorraine Swanson. 21 - Valdimir Vasiltvich. 23 - Vladimir Vasiltvich.

Images are courtesy of Shutterstock.com. With thanks to Getty Images, Thinkstock Photo, and iStockphoto.

All facts, statistics, web addresses, and URLs in this book were verified as valid and accurate at time of writing.
No responsibility for any changes to external websites or references can be accepted by either the author or publisher.

CONTENTS

Words that look like **this** can be found in the glossary on page 24.

LET'S PLAY ICE HOCKEY!

Have you ever wondered about the math, angles, and **forces** behind the game of ice hockey? Grab your skates, stick, and helmet, because the puck is about to drop!

Each ice hockey team is allowed six players on the ice rink at any one time. Two teams play against each other to try to get the puck in the other team's goal.

THE RIGHT RINK

Ice hockey rinks can have different surface **textures** depending on the temperature of the ice.

Colder ice is harder and has a smoother texture. Warmer ice is softer and has a rougher texture.

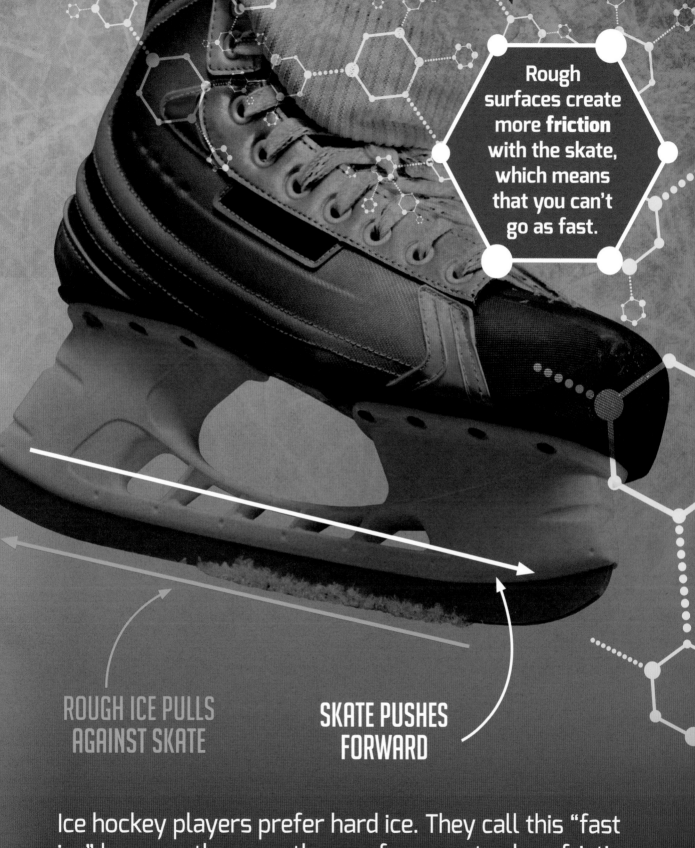

Rough surfaces create more **friction** with the skate, which means that you can't go as fast.

ROUGH ICE PULLS AGAINST SKATE

SKATE PUSHES FORWARD

Ice hockey players prefer hard ice. They call this "fast ice" because the smoother surface creates less friction between the skate and the ice.

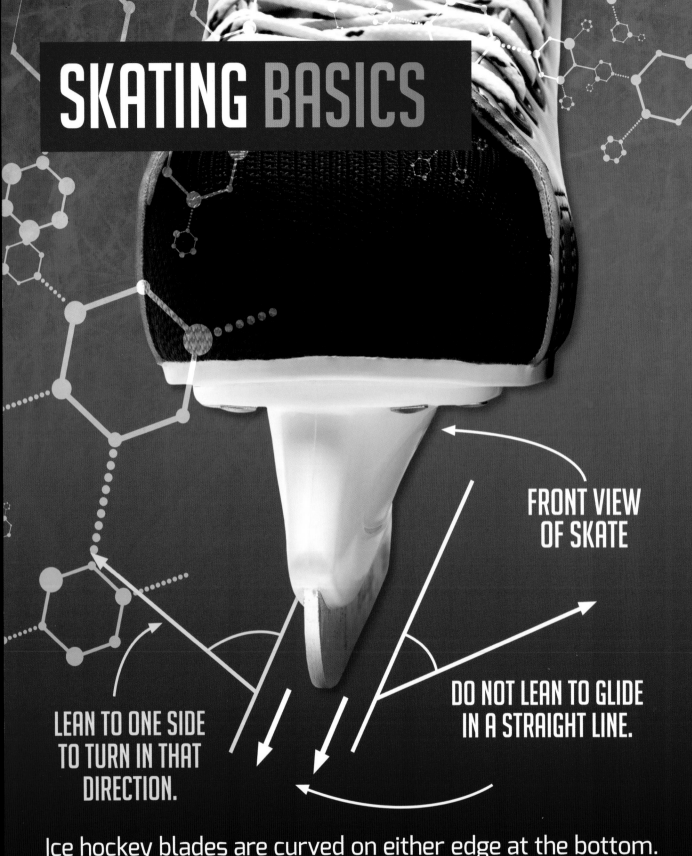

SKATING BASICS

FRONT VIEW OF SKATE

DO NOT LEAN TO GLIDE IN A STRAIGHT LINE.

LEAN TO ONE SIDE TO TURN IN THAT DIRECTION.

Ice hockey blades are curved on either edge at the bottom. This is so you can travel and turn very quickly.

To travel forward as fast as you can, you need to position one of your feet at a 45-degree angle. Don't forget to bend your knees to create more speed.

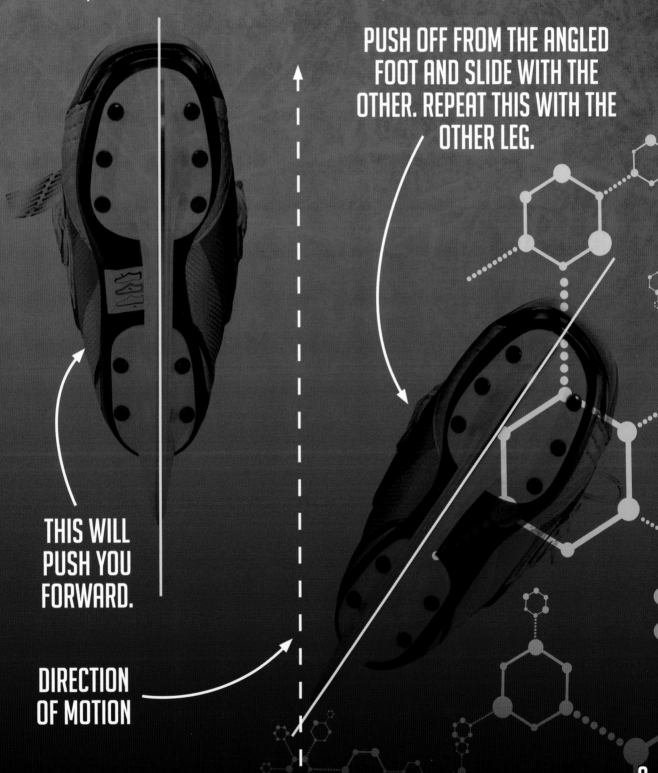

PUSH OFF FROM THE ANGLED FOOT AND SLIDE WITH THE OTHER. REPEAT THIS WITH THE OTHER LEG.

THIS WILL PUSH YOU FORWARD.

DIRECTION OF MOTION

PERFECT PASSING

Ice hockey is a very speedy sport, and everything happens very quickly. To be able to make the perfect pass, you need to think quickly about how your teammate is traveling.

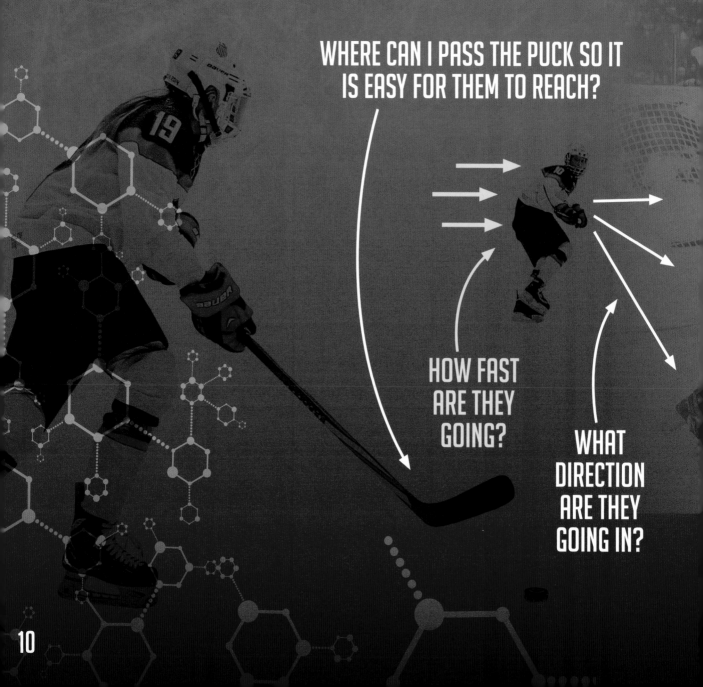

WHERE CAN I PASS THE PUCK SO IT IS EASY FOR THEM TO REACH?

HOW FAST ARE THEY GOING?

WHAT DIRECTION ARE THEY GOING IN?

The farther you bring back your stick before hitting, the more **momentum** you will build up and the faster the puck will go.

The faster your teammate is traveling, the harder you'll need to hit the puck so it reaches them in time.

Thinking carefully about all these things will help you push the puck into the space your teammate will be in after you have hit the puck.

BOUNCE IT OFF THE BOARD

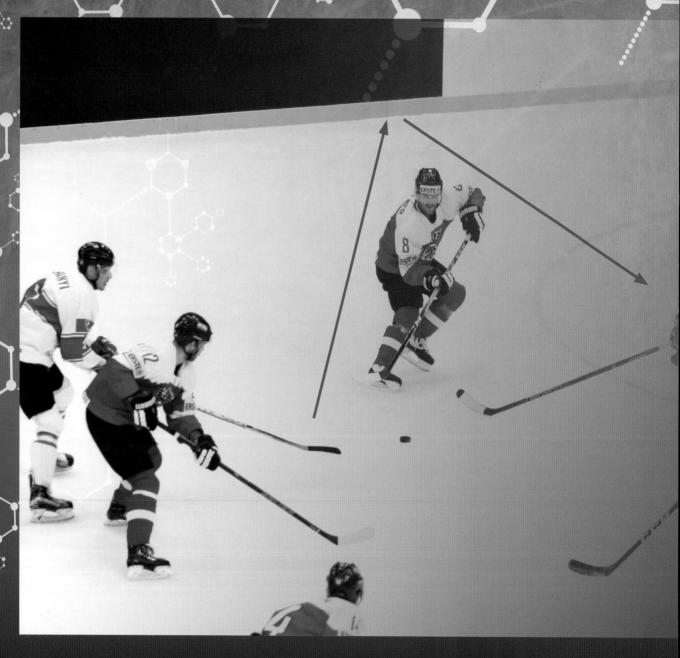

If you can't see a player to pass to, you can bounce the puck off of the boards along the side of the rink. This will help you get around the other team's players.

The angle at which the puck hits the board is the same as the angle at which it will **ricochet** off it. The smaller the angle, the farther forward the puck will travel. Hard hits create more force, making the puck travel faster. Softer hits have less force, and the puck will travel slower.

After you've hit the puck, swerve around to get past your **opponent!**

SCORE A SLAP SHOT

Slap shots are all about building up energy and transferring it to the puck. The slap shot is the fastest shot in ice hockey.

SWING YOUR STICK FROM HIGH UP TO BUILD MOMENTUM.

TRANSFER YOUR WEIGHT FROM YOUR BACK LEG TO YOUR FRONT LEG TO PUT MORE ENERGY INTO YOUR SWING.

THE PUCK WILL RECEIVE ALL OF THE ENERGY YOU HAVE BUILT UP AND TRAVEL IN THE DIRECTION OF YOUR HIT.

As the puck shoots through the air, lots of forces are acting upon it.

AIR RESISTANCE PUSHES AGAINST THE PUCK.

Hit the puck as hard as you can so that the puck has enough energy to reach the net before it is slowed down by air resistance and gravity.

ENERGY PUSHES THE PUCK FORWARD.

GRAVITY PULLS THE PUCK DOWNWARD.

A WINNING WRIST SHOT

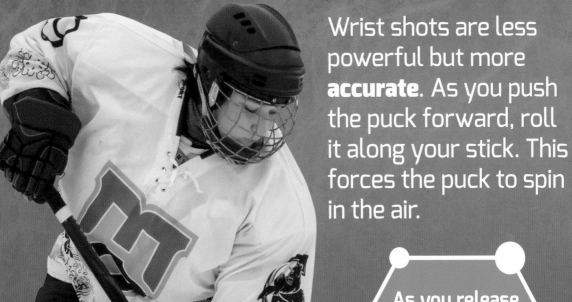

Wrist shots are less powerful but more **accurate**. As you push the puck forward, roll it along your stick. This forces the puck to spin in the air.

As you release the puck from your stick, curve your stick over it to push it at the correct angle.

ROTATE BLADE AROUND PUCK

ROLL PUCK ALONG BLADE

The puck has a cylindrical (say: sih-LIN-drih-cul) shape. This means that when it is spun into the air, it doesn't curve; instead, the spin keeps it going in the direction it was hit.

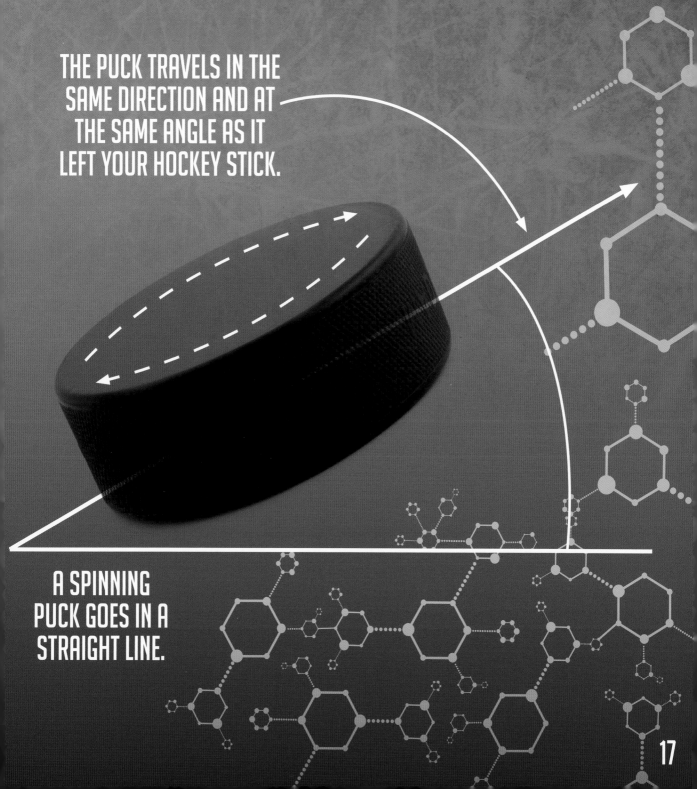

THE PUCK TRAVELS IN THE SAME DIRECTION AND AT THE SAME ANGLE AS IT LEFT YOUR HOCKEY STICK.

A SPINNING PUCK GOES IN A STRAIGHT LINE.

COLLISIONS!

Hockey is a **contact sport**, which means that players are always bumping into each other. When this happens, lots of energy is transferred in lots of different directions.

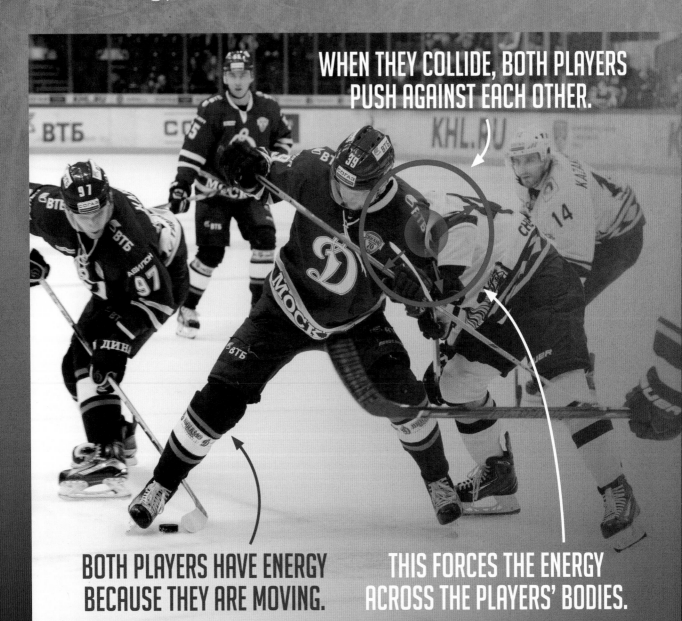

WHEN THEY COLLIDE, BOTH PLAYERS PUSH AGAINST EACH OTHER.

BOTH PLAYERS HAVE ENERGY BECAUSE THEY ARE MOVING.

THIS FORCES THE ENERGY ACROSS THE PLAYERS' BODIES.

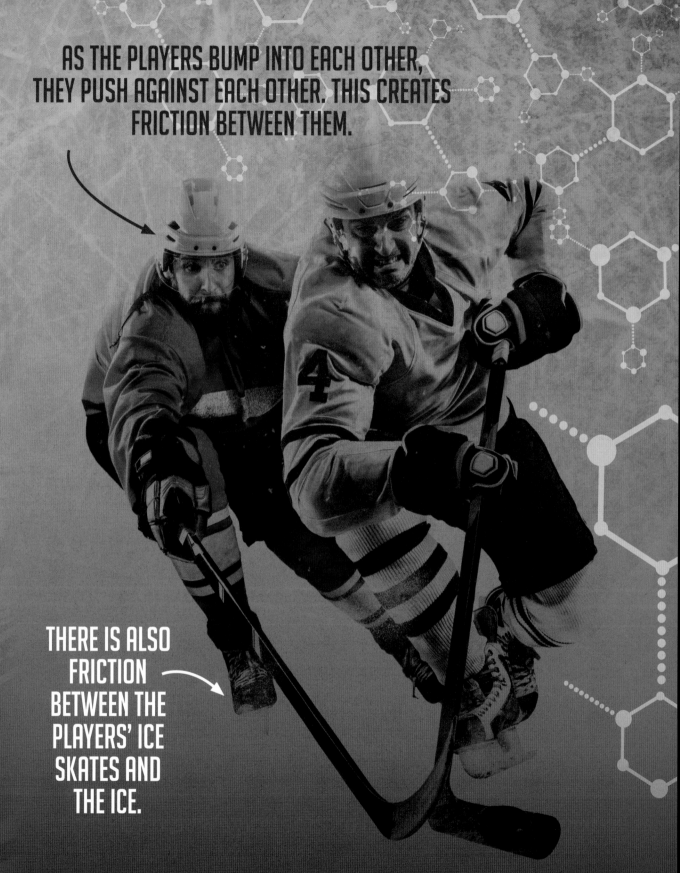

AS THE PLAYERS BUMP INTO EACH OTHER, THEY PUSH AGAINST EACH OTHER. THIS CREATES FRICTION BETWEEN THEM.

THERE IS ALSO FRICTION BETWEEN THE PLAYERS' ICE SKATES AND THE ICE.

When players collide, lots of friction is created.

SAVE IT!

This goaltender is taking up most of the space of the goal with his body, pads, and stick. This gives him a good chance of stopping the puck from going into the net.

As an ice hockey goaltender, you need to make sure you are taking up as much of the goal's **area** as possible.

As a goaltender, you need to know where a player is most likely to strike. Where in the net do you think this player is going to aim for? Is it number 1, 2, 3, or 4?

SPOT THE PUCK

That's right, it's number 2! Let's take a closer look and see the science behind the shot.

SPACE

The player will shoot where there is the most space so that the goaltender is less likely to save it. This player will shoot to the right of the goaltender.

HEIGHT AND OBSTACLES

The player in this shot will flick the puck up in the air so that it hits the top-right corner of the net. This is because it is the farthest away from obstacles such as the goaltender's arms, legs, and stick.

GLOSSARY

accurate   precise and careful
area   the amount of surface somewhere
                      or something has
contact sport   a sport where players' bodies are allowed
                      to touch
force   a push or pull of an object
friction   when two objects rub against each other
momentum   the force an object has when it is moving,
                      based on its speed and weight
opponent   someone playing or working against you
resistance   a force pushing back against something
ricochet   to bounce off of something at an angle
texture   how something feels

INDEX

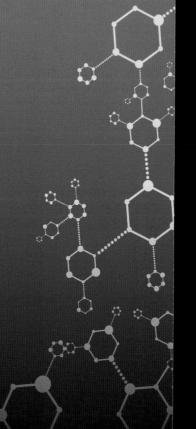